EMPTY YOUR CUP

Why We Have Low Self-Esteem and

How Mindfulness Can Help

Yong Kang Chan
www.nerdycreator.com

Your Free Gifts

Low self-esteem can cause problems in your work, relationship, and mental health. After my episode of depression, I realize the importance of loving myself. So I've put together these three free gifts for you.

1. Self-Love Quiz

Do you love yourself unconditionally? Or are you too hard on yourself? I had created this quiz to help you find out how much you love yourself.

2. The Round Moon

Being an introvert, I found it challenging to fit in sometimes. This short story was written to encourage us to embrace our differences and accept ourselves.

3. Self-Love Project

This project is a compilation of 44 self-love articles I had written over a year. It includes topics such as:

- forgiving yourself
- setting boundaries
- overcoming negative self-criticism
- letting go of expectations
- being authentic, and more.

If you would like to receive any of the gifts for free, please download them at www.nerdycreator.com/self-love-gifts.

CONTENTS

WHY DID I WRITE THIS BOOK?

Why don't I love myself? This was the question I had been pondering for years. On the surface, I knew I should be happy. I had all the reasons to love my life. I did well in school. I had just graduated from a local university and found a decent job in an auditing firm. I had friends and I got along well with my colleagues. There wasn't any argument or animosity. Family life was good, too. I had a complete family. I couldn't ask for more.

I should love myself, right? But that wasn't the case.

Since I was a kid, I had experienced low self-esteem. I felt uncomfortable and awkward in social situations. I thought I would outgrow it eventually, but I hadn't.

Eight years ago, I found myself hiding and crying in the toilet cubicle at the office during lunch, still feeling the same unworthiness and disconnection from the world. My communication skills had improved, but my self-esteem was still the same, low. No matter how hard I tried to love myself, I still felt that I wasn't good enough. No matter how well I got along with my peers, I still felt excluded, an outsider, and even when I knew I was worthy of love and had evidence to back it up, I didn't believe it.

Why is this so?

Why am I not able to love myself unconditionally?

Why do I always feel inferior to others?

Why is there a voice in my head that keeps telling me I'm not good enough?

The culprit is the mind.

This book was inspired by my own experience with low self-esteem and the books I've read. It is a result of looking back at my life after I thought I had overcome depression. I was lying in bed one day, reflecting on how much I had changed over time, and I saw a pattern. So I quickly plotted a timeline of my life on a piece of paper and, suddenly, I had an image of a cup. At that instant, I knew I had to use the cup as an analogy for this book.

If you are looking for something technical, complex, or extensively researched, this might not be the book for you. I tend to keep my writing simple and let it speak to the soul. I didn't write this because I am an expert in psychology. Neither am I trying to get you to believe in spirituality. This book was written so you can begin your own exploration and reflection.

You have probably heard or read about the classic Zen story on "emptying your cup." The Zen master keeps pouring tea into the visitor's cup even though it's already full to the brim. I hope you read this book with an open and "empty" mind, too. Don't take my words for the total truth. Check them against your personal experience and see how much truth they hold for you.

Enjoy!

Yong Kang Chan
Singapore
2017

Introduction

I THOUGHT I LOVED MYSELF

When asked to make a list of everything we love about ourselves, most of us would be able to write something, even if we hate ourselves or have low self-esteem. When I was a teen, this was my first self-esteem exercise. After suffering from low self-esteem for years, someone from an online forum suggested I list ten things I love about myself. I did and it felt good...

For a while.

Soon, I was back to my usual habits of belittling myself: *No one likes me. I am boring. No one wants to listen or talk to me.* Every time I saw other students chatting and having a good time, I felt alone. Every time I was with my friends and they were chatting happily without me, I felt left out. When I was asked a question and it was my turn to speak up, I couldn't. I stumbled and didn't know what to say. The thoughts in my head were perfectly coherent, but once they came out of my mouth nothing sounded right. I enjoyed studying and learning new things, but I can't say I liked school very much. When it came to social situations, I felt awkward and uncomfortable.

This went on for years. I felt inferior and unworthy every single day, but somehow I survived. Writing down my feelings and thoughts helped, and because I was getting better at communicating with others, I didn't see my low self-esteem as a problem. I just thought that one day I would be as confident as everyone else and I would feel better about myself...

But, of course, I didn't.

After graduation, I began my first job as an auditor. I soon realized that working life was much worse than school life, especially during lunch. It was okay when we were at the client's place. We would go out and have lunch together as a team. But when we were back in the office, everyone seemed to have his or her own clique. A few times, I found myself alone in an empty office during lunch. Everyone had gone out and I was either uninvited or forgotten. This might sound silly now, in hindsight. I could have asked my colleagues if I could join for lunch. But at that time, I was so afraid of being rejected by others. *What if they don't want me to join them? Wouldn't I be imposing on them?*

The truth was that I hated lunch. *But why was having lunch so difficult?* I didn't even dare to go out for lunch alone. If my colleagues had forgotten to invite me and they saw me eating alone in a restaurant, it would be awkward for all of us. On the flip side, if they had no intention of asking me out for lunch, and they caught me eating lunch alone, I would be perceived as a loser with no other friends to dine with. So at times like this, I had to sneak into a nearby eatery and ask for takeaway, or walk a long distance to the outskirts of the financial district so I wouldn't bump into my colleagues. Sometimes, when I wasn't in the mood, I would hide in one of the office toilet cubicles and skip lunch altogether.

Finally, one day, I broke down in a toilet cubicle. What was a 25-year-old man like me doing hiding in the bathroom, afraid of having lunch? I was so ashamed of myself. But it turned out to be a good thing, because it helped me realize I needed to change my life and myself.

The next six years were great. I left my auditing job and became an accountant. I started watching videos and reading self-help books on overcoming low self-esteem, building confidence, and being positive. I purchased online courses that helped me change my negative beliefs about myself. My self-esteem improved tremendously and I became more confident in life and my work. I even wrote my first book, *Fearless Passion*, and later became an animator.

Life was great. I loved myself…

Or so I thought.

If you have read my memoir, *The Emotional Gift*, you probably know what happened next: I suffered depression after I didn't get a job I had been initially promised. But being jobless wasn't the problem. The incident brought out the undesirable emotions I had felt for myself in the past. The negative thoughts that had gone missing for the previous six years were all back. It was as though they had been lurking in the background, waiting for an opportunity to attack me. Once I faltered, I was lost. Streams of negative thoughts flooded my mind and I sank back into depression.

During those six years of bliss, I thought I had everything figured out.

I thought I had gotten rid of my low self-esteem for good.

I thought I finally loved myself completely.

But no, I didn't.

It only took one small challenge in life to crumble my self-esteem.

So… why is our self-esteem so vulnerable?

It's All About Perception

Low self-esteem is the *belief* that we are not good or worthy enough. It's a self-perception. It doesn't matter how successful or confident you are. You can be wealthy, beautiful, or well liked by others and still don't feel good about yourself. The way other people perceive you doesn't affect your self-esteem. It's how you perceive yourself that matters.

Basically, there are two types of low self-esteem. The first type is the chronic, depressive kind. You hate yourself no matter what you do, or not do. You have negative thoughts about yourself and you beat yourself up all the time.

The second type is condition-based. Your self-esteem depends on your competency, approval from others, or something you attach your self-worth to.

The first type is easily recognizable because it's so extreme. People in the first group know they have low self-esteem. But most of us who have low self-esteem belong to the second group, which isn't as obvious. People in this group don't consciously *think* they are bad. But when something doesn't go their way, or they are denied the approval of others, they subconsciously *feel* they are unworthy or inferior.

People who have low self-esteem
might not even know they have low self-esteem.

For example, during most of my time in school I had low self-esteem and I knew it. But when I started working, I thought my self-esteem had improved because my confidence and communication skills had improved. Not knowing that I had attached my feelings of self-worth to my work, when the work was gone so was my self-esteem and I became depressed.

This kind of high self-esteem is not really high self-esteem. It's temporary and based on conditions. Deep down inside our subconscious, we still believe we are not good enough. The feeling of unworthiness is still there, even though we feel more positive and confident in our abilities. We realize our high self-esteem is a facade when the conditions that validate our self-worth are gone.

How, then, do we change our self-perception from within?

Solving the Real Problem

Even though low self-esteem is a perception problem, it's not about changing our perception of ourselves. It's about changing the place from which we perceive ourselves. What's the difference?

If we are watching a standing concert and someone in front of us blocks our view, we don't change our perception of the concert. The concert didn't become less enjoyable because we don't get to see it. It's still the same concert. Instead of changing our perception of the concert, what we are most likely to do is move to a better position from which to view the concert.

However, when it comes to self-esteem, what do most of us do instead?

First, we try to change ourselves. We believe that by making ourselves better, more confident and more successful, we can change the way we perceive ourselves. But this doesn't work in the long run, because it's not what we believe deep down inside. Our belief system controls our self-perception. Feeling inferior has already become a habit. You can't change this feeling without first changing your beliefs. (More on this later in Chapter 3.)

Second, we try to change our self-beliefs into something more positive. Changing the way we habitually think can help us reduce negative thoughts and feelings towards ourselves. This is a great concept, and it helped me for six good years. However, the mind is complex. Unless we can go inside the mind and identify our beliefs, one by one (like in a filing cabinet), we are bound to miss some and we won't be able to change all of them.

You can't find love inside your mind.
That's not where love is.

Furthermore, changing our self-beliefs doesn't solve the real problem. As mentioned in the concert analogy above, the problem doesn't lie with our beliefs or us. We are unable to love ourselves because we perceive ourselves from an undesirable position — the mind's perspective. The mind is good for many things, such as judging, analyzing, and comparing. But we can't find love there. The mind only understands love from a conceptual point of view.

In fact, the mind creates our suffering, our negative thoughts, and emotions. If I were to tell myself: *No one likes me*, I might still have a tingling feeling in my body. My mind has memorized the pain and stored it away in my body. All it needs is a trigger to activate the pain and I will feel the hurt again. Seeking love in the mind is like seeking love from the creator of your own drama. The mind cannot give us what we are looking for.

If we are able to shift our position to the spirit's perspective, the view will be vastly different. We can only find peace, joy, and love in the spirit. Viewing yourself from the spirit's perspective allows you to be detached from the drama in your mind. Then, you will realize your current self-perception is none other than a mental image created by your mind.

This is what mindfulness and this book are all about — shifting the place of perception from the mind to the spirit.

The Seven Stages of the Cup

The purpose of this book is to help you become empty of everything you believe to be true about yourself and reconnect with your spiritual self. It's to help you distinguish between your mind's image of who you are (referred to as "the ego" by most) and your true spiritual self. Hopefully, with this awareness you will continue to practice mindfulness and stay in touch with the love that you are.

Throughout this book, I'll be using the cup as an analogy for the mind, and I've divided the cup's journey into seven stages as follows:

- Stage 1 - Empty
- Stage 2 - Influence
- Stage 3 - Beliefs
- Stage 4 - Identity
- Stage 5 - Judge
- Stage 6 - Awakening
- Stage 7 - Mastery

Unless you have read psychology books, you might not be aware of the first three stages. Reading the first three chapters will give you a basic understanding of how the mind works and how we become who we are in present time.

Most of us will be able to relate to the fourth and fifth stages, when the mind is the most active and developed. But not all of us are aware of how it affects our lives.

Our awakening occurs in the sixth stage. At this stage, we realize the distinction between our ego and our spiritual self. The last stage is not final, but rather an invitation to stay conscious of your spiritual self through practice.

At the end of each chapter, I've also included a little exercise to help you understand each stage better. All of these exercises are designed to help you become more aware.

So let's begin this journey together, each with an empty cup.

THE SEVEN STAGES OF THE CUP

Stage 1

EMPTY

Have you ever wondered what makes babies so attractive?

Whenever there's a baby around, everyone focuses his or her attention on the baby. They crowd around the baby just to see it sleep and yawn. They try to make the baby laugh and take turns carrying the baby.

Most people think it's their physical attributes that attract everyone to babies because they have such cute features. They have eyes that are too big for their heads, and heads that are too big for their bodies. They have short, flabby limbs, and cute, tiny fingers and toes. But are these the real reasons newborns are so lovable?

When babies cry as loud as they possibly can, do you still find them cute? Sure, they still have those big eyes and tiny fingers. But when they are screaming, they are viewed as "little monsters." They disrupt your sleep, drive you nuts, and use up the personal time you so desperately needed.

So how can it be their physical attributes that make them lovable?

The answer to this question is simple: babies are beautiful because their minds are empty. They are filled with the peace, joy, and innocence that we find so desirable. We are irresistibly drawn to them when they are sleeping soundly, when they are looking around in awe with their big round eyes, and when they are laughing for no reason other than their joy at being alive. We are also attracted to their presence because it's familiar. We were all babies once, and we existed in the same peaceful, joy-filled state. In fact, we have it now, even though it might have been long forgotten or covered up by our mental noise.

The Beauty of Emptiness

Shape clay into a vessel;
It is the space within that makes it useful.
Carve fine doors and windows,
But the room is useful in its emptiness.
Lao Tzu, Tao Te Ching

A cup is always made to be empty. It's only when it's empty that it is useful. Just like a cup, our minds are made to be empty. Each of us was blessed with an empty mind at birth. As newborns, we had zero knowledge. Everything was new to us, and we were in awe of everything we saw and experienced. Emptiness defines the first stage of the mind.

Do you remember the first time you heard a voice in your head? When you were a baby, there were no such voices. There were sounds and images, but they didn't stay in your mind for long. At this stage, you didn't know any words, so you had no thoughts — and without any thoughts, there is no suffering.

Imagine this: If you don't have any thoughts or narratives in your head, will you still feel unworthy? Will you still be self-critical and ashamed of yourself? Will you continue to compare yourself unfavorably to others?

Unlike adults, babies perceive things around them as they are. They do not judge anything. If they are uncomfortable, they cry for help. If they are hungry, again, they cry for help. They can't express themselves with words, so they cry as loud as they can to get help.

But don't mistake the crying of a baby as an expression of misery. Babies are never miserable. Once their needs are met, they let it go. They stop crying. They don't hold on to grudges, even if their parents don't feed them on time.

Babies never let their minds get filled up with negativity.

Nothingness is the most peaceful state of mind.

There's no unworthiness or inferiority.

There's only pure love.

The peace we experience when being with a baby is rarely seen among adults. We might experience stress, problems, and shame, but we seldom feel peaceful in adulthood. We have so much information in our minds that we judge everything, including ourselves. We might even feel guilty about not taking good care of our babies.

Babies have no such judgment or worries. When their parents are thinking how cute or noisy they are, they think nothing of themselves. Babies don't judge themselves as being good or bad. They don't care if they are beautiful, or not. They don't care if they are being too loud, or not. They just cry when they want something, sleep when they are tired, and spit up milk when they need to.

Adults, on the other hand, continue to eat even when they are full because they feel they should not waste food, or it would be impolite to reject food someone has offered them. Some people starve themselves to stay thin because they care so much about their appearance and how others might judge them.

Babies don't hate any aspect of themselves. They care only about their well-being enough to get their needs met. This is self-love, and it's also the beauty of having an empty mind.

The Burden of a Complex Mind

The great thing about being human is that we have complex minds. But the unfortunate thing about being human is also having a complex mind. There's a price to pay for being able to analyze, determine meanings, feel emotions, and communicate with language. With the mind comes psychological suffering and emotional pain.

Without the mind, the idea

of worthiness would not exist.

When we see our friends talking happily with each other, we would not be so likely to conclude that we are boring or unlikable if it wasn't for our thoughts. The mind suggests that our friends would rather be with someone other than us. When we achieve success at work, we wouldn't continue to feel like a failure if our minds didn't compare us with someone more successful. What about when we are happily in love, but we sabotage our relationships by creating doubts.

Similar to babies, animals don't have self-esteem problems. When animals are hungry, they eat. The pig doesn't think: *I'm fat. I shouldn't eat any more food*, or *When will I stop being such a glutton?* Pigs eat until they feel full. When there's danger, they run. Deer never view themselves as cowards in front of tigers. To them, it's all a matter of survival.

Unlike us, animals don't care too much about what their peers think of them. Their minds do not give them an identity to uphold. They just do what comes naturally.

This doesn't mean that we should get rid of our complex mind or live like an animal or a baby. We don't get our needs met by crying like babies once we become adults. Behavior expectations for adults are infinitely higher than for babies.

Moreover, the mind is useful to us in many ways. We can strive to hold the content in our minds lightly and not get too carried away by our thoughts and emotions. Learning to be mindful can be of great help. We can return to our original, empty state by unlearning some of the things we learned in childhood, especially the false beliefs we accepted about ourselves.

The Fear of Being Emptied

Have you ever tried meditation? Instead of quieting the mind, sometimes the mind gets louder and noisier: *This won't work! Give it up. How long am I going to sit here?*

Letting go of our thoughts, emotions, and beliefs can be challenging, at first. The content in the mind is like our possessions. Even if these false beliefs are of no value to us, the mind still clings to them because we are afraid we might need them someday; our beliefs become a mental habit. This is what economists and behavioral scientists call the "sunk cost fallacy." [1]

Initially, I rewrote this book four times, because every time I sat down to research and write I discovered new information. But my mind refused to let go of the old content. I kept thinking I should keep everything I had written so far because it might be useful for later. As a result, the book became messy and cluttered. It was hard to press the "delete" button because I had spent so much effort and time writing some of the paragraphs. Just the press of a button and within seconds, the words would be erased. Fortunately, I was able to resolve this issue and complete the writing.

The mind is wired to hold onto things for survival purposes.

---

[1] The "sunk cost fallacy" refers to a misconception: You make rational decisions based on the future value of objects, investments, and experiences. The Truth: Your decisions are tainted by the emotional investments you accumulate, and the more you invest in something the harder it becomes to abandon it.

Emptiness is a scary place for the mind.

It loses power when it is emptied.

The mind resists being emptied because we are afraid of losing mental control. When we get caught up in our thoughts and emotions, the mind gets our attention. When it is emptied, it loses our attention and it makes something up (sometimes unpleasant content) to get our attention again. The mind equates emptiness with boredom or stupidity, and it makes us think that staying busy is important. But the trade-off is our joy and peace.

Wouldn't it be nice to be like a baby again? No worries, no thoughts, so peaceful and carefree. Unfortunately, none of us gets to remain a baby. This innocent state is short-lived, and social conditioning and the people around us eventually fill our personal cups.

Exercise: Observe a Baby

If you have the opportunity, observe a baby. The spirit of a baby is the most visible because it isn't affected by any mental noise. Observe the baby when it's sleeping or when it's interacting with someone else or the environment. Can you feel the same peace within you, too? Does it resonate with you? Also, notice how quickly the emotions of the baby change when the baby's needs are met.

Now, observe your mind for 5 to 15 minutes. Can you relax into a quiet space like a baby?

Stage 2

INFLUENCE

"I don't want orange juice," the child argues, as the mom pours the juice into the child's cup.

"But orange juice is good for you. It has a lot of vitamin C," the mom says, as she continues to pour the juice into her child's cup.

"No!" the child says. He takes his cup away. He is adamant that he will not drink something he hates. "I don't want orange juice. I want a soda!" he says.

The mom's face darkens, "If you don't bring your cup

over to me, there will be no television for you tonight." The child reluctantly brings his cup over and lets his parent pours juice into his cup. Even though he hates orange juice, he's not going to sacrifice his television time for it.

You don't get to choose
what goes into your cup.

Previously, during the first stage, we learned that a baby does not know how to use its mind, because the baby's mind is so empty the baby doesn't even know it exists. Now, at the second stage, we begin to learn about influence. The minds get filled up quickly as we get older — not by us, but by the people closest to us, our parents, grandparents, and other caretakers.

When we were children, we didn't get to choose what we wanted to learn. Our parents made these decisions for us. If our parents served us juice, then we had juice. If they served us tea, then we drank tea. Even if we didn't like what we were given, we obeyed our parents because we needed them for love and survival. Without them, we would have no food, no shelter, and no toys. We wouldn't have been able to survive on our own in this world if it wasn't for our parents.

Our self-worth depends very much on what type of "mental content" we receive. If we come from a loving family with positive attitudes, we will be likely to develop a good sense of self-esteem. But if we come from an abusive family background in which our parents argued all the time, or they didn't give us enough encouragement, love, and attention, then we will probably find it more challenging to love ourselves.

There's nothing much we can do about it. This is part of growing up. We were not in control; our parents were. They had a strong influence over us. They shaped who we were in the first few years of our lives. Sometimes, growing up can make us feel powerless — but this chapter isn't about changing the past.

What's more important is to understand how our childhood experiences influenced and shaped our current self-perception so we can break the connection.

How Do Childhood Experiences Influence Adult Self-Perception?

Most of us don't remember much of our childhood before the age of seven. But this doesn't mean our minds do not remember. Implicit memory, a type of long-term memory, doesn't require conscious thinking. Emotions felt in childhood can be deeply embedded in the subconscious part of the brain, even though we don't recall the events that caused the emotions.

You might not think too much about your childhood experiences. But don't underestimate the influence your parents had on you during childhood. When you were little and you looked up at these giants who were your parents, you thought they knew everything. Anything they did, even unintentionally, could affect your self-esteem and how you perceive yourself. Understanding the association between the two can help you unlock the limiting self-beliefs that have been holding you back for years.

Here are five childhood events or circumstances that might have affected your self-esteem:

1. An adverse physical environment for growth.

Probably the most obvious influence is your immediate environment. If you spent most of your childhood in conflict, war, and natural disaster, or if you experienced traumatic events such as abuse or the sudden loss of a parent, your self-worth is going to be affected.

A child who has experienced abuse will tend to blame him or herself for what happened, even though it was not their fault. We trust our parents more than anyone else. As children, we saw them every day and had close contact with them. They provided us with food, shelter, and love. As children, we don't think our parents will harm us, so when something goes wrong we think it's our fault.

Parents going through a divorce usually leave the children feeling powerless, too. As much as they might want to keep their parents together, children know they have no power over such situations. Some feel they are responsible for their parents' divorce. Some believe that if they had only been more obedient or quieter, their parents would not have separated.

Even small accidents, such as a child falling off the sofa, can create a chain of negative emotions if not handled properly. One parent might scold the other parent for being negligent. The parent at fault might feel guilty about being inattentive and create unnecessary psychological distance between themselves and the children. This can result in the children thinking they are the cause of their parents' arguments. These feelings can continue into adulthood at the unconscious level and affect the way we see ourselves.

2. One or both of our parents don't love themselves.

Children learn by copying what their parents do and say. Some pretend to be cooking like their mom does in the kitchen. Others use swear words they have learned from their parents to get their parents' attention. When we are children, our minds are like fertile land that is ready to absorb everything our five senses pick up — whether it's something our parents want us to learn, or not.

However, it's not the parents' actions and words that matter the most. Children are sensitive to their parents' emotions, too. They might not know how to communicate what they feel in words, but they share their parents' happiness and unhappiness. Even if the parents are hiding their emotions or pretending to be happy, children are able to sense it. They can tell when their parents are trying to teach them something they don't practice themselves.

If you have parents who don't feel good about themselves, can you understand how you might have emulated their behaviors? Our parents are our first role models. Even if your parents did their best to give you unconditional love but they do not love themselves, a part of you will want to share their pain. When we observed our parents criticizing themselves and each other, we might have accepted it as "proper" behavior and done the same: continue criticizing ourselves into adulthood.

3. Physical and emotional absence of parents.

Some parents are never physically around. It's very likely that both of your parents were working when you were young, and you were taken care by your grandparents, relatives, or a domestic helper instead. As children, we might feel neglected because we do not understand why our parents need to work and earn a living.

Sometimes, it's not the physical absence; it's the emotional absence. Parents might be physically present with their children, but they are emotionally unavailable. Perhaps they are busy with their work or watching television, and they are only pretending to listen to the child. Children who are just learning how to speak tend to be very talkative and inquisitive. Parents who don't understand this can become annoyed with the endless questions and shut their children out. They simply stop listening, sometimes unintentionally, as they've had a tough day at work.

During childhood, we need care and attention the most. When our parents are unable to be there for us, when we most need their love, we feel insignificant, unimportant, and unloved. Unfortunately, these feelings can stay with us, even after we grow up.

4. Preconceived parenting beliefs.

A few years ago, my colleague brought her baby to the office. The baby was crying loudly, but she and her husband refused to pick him up and comfort him. Both of them believed that if they picked up their son too often he would become spoiled and want to be carried all the time. Some colleagues agreed.

I wasn't a parent myself, so I didn't say anything. But somehow I felt uncomfortable with this idea. Before I was 25 years old, I always thought my parents didn't love me. When I was a child, I used to wish they could hug me and encourage me more, but they never did. They might have felt withholding love and praise was the right thing to do, but it only made me feel that I didn't deserve to be loved. This lack of affection is partially why I grew feeling insecure and unloved.

I'm thankful, however, that my parents didn't scold or beat me when I was young. Some parents believe that scolding and beating their children is the way to discipline them. They believe children are inherently naughty and need to be taught how to behave. But often, young children are just testing what they can or cannot do. One-year-old children might throw objects around seemingly without any real purpose. They are not being naughty or trying to spite you. They are just practicing their newfound skill of dropping and releasing objects.

If your parents lost their temper and yelled at you, or if they told you repeatedly that you were "bad" (or you had some other negative quality), it will be very difficult for you to feel good about yourself as an adult.

5. Our parents' expectations.

Other than preconceived parenting beliefs, your parents might have had certain beliefs and expectations of you that affected your self-perception. For example, your parents might have insisted that you look and dress a certain way to look beautiful, or they might have compared you with other siblings, which caused you to feel rejected.

Also, some parents are not very patient when it comes to teaching. When their children don't understand something after being told a few times, they get frustrated easily and say something like, "Why can't you get this right?" Out of frustration, perhaps they give up and conclude that you are not good in mathematics or grammar. Even if they don't say so, their unreasonable expectations can make you feel stupid, as though you are not good enough for them.

For some children, pleasing their parents and meeting their expectations are of utmost importance. If they can't please their parents, they start asking why, and then they feel bad about themselves for disappointing their parents.

Why Shouldn't We Blame Our Parents?

It's easy to blame our parents after we come to know how they have damaged our self-esteem, but that shouldn't be the case.

Most parents do the best they can in raising their children.

It's important to realize that most of your parents' beliefs came from their parents, your grandparents. Someone else also influenced them heavily, and they might not be aware of it. If they had known better, they most likely wouldn't have done the same to you. Instead of blaming your parents for their mistakes, be the person who stops the cycle. Don't let the next generation suffer the same fate as you.

Furthermore, if you are the first-born child, the number of years your parents have been parents is the same as your age. Even though parents usually think they know more than their children, they are actually new to parenting when they start out with their first baby. They spend the same amount of time learning to be parents as we spend learning about life. Most of them didn't go to school to learn about parenting or have access to the resources we have now.

We can learn to be more forgiving towards our parents, because parenting is an ongoing, life-long learning process. There is so much to be learned. Plus, resenting someone doesn't make us happy. So why hold onto negativity?

You have no choice about what gets poured into your cup, but you have a choice as to what you accept and believe.

Finally, even though we didn't have the choice to choose what content went into our cups, our minds have assigned negative meanings to these past events. So we are partly responsible for our own low self-esteem.

In the next chapter, you will see that we have the ability to choose what to believe. Our parents didn't force us to think negative thoughts about ourselves. Even if they wanted to, they couldn't. The difference lies in the fact that we are unaware of the choices we made as children.

Exercise: Reflect on Your Childhood

Spend 15 to 30 minutes to reflect on your childhood. How does your childhood affect your self-esteem and perception of yourself today? Write down any events that might have influenced you when you were a child. You might not be able to remember them in detail. You might have experienced similar events when you were much older. Write them down, too.

Also, reflect on your relationships with your parents. If you are still holding resentment for them, are you able to forgive them — right now? If you can, that's great. But if you can't, don't force it. Just come back to this exercise at another time.

Stage 3

BELIEFS

Words have no meaning to children. Take the words, "Don't run around the house!" as an example. In hindsight, as an adult, you know running around the house recklessly can cause injuries. You know where your parents were coming from. But as a child, did you understand why?

Young children don't understand why they are not allowed to run around freely, even if their parents explain it to them. All they know is that their parents are restricting their freedom. They don't understand the concept of injury until they injure themselves and experience pain.

The ability to give meaning to our experiences can be the beginning of our negative self-talk.

When we were young, our parents taught us how to speak and read. But once we learned words and their meanings, we would never be the same again. We started to have thoughts and began to lose the innocence we had when we were babies. We started to understand the difference between tall and short, small and big, beautiful and ugly, right and wrong, and good and bad. We gradually became mired in duality.

Once we understand these concepts, the mind wants to judge, tell stories, and assign meaning to every single event we experience, including ourselves. When our parents scold us, we don't just *feel* unloved; we *believe* we are worthless. Furthermore, if we keep having the same repetitive thoughts about ourselves and feel strongly about the events involved, our thoughts become beliefs.

Beliefs mark the beginning of the third stage, the stage at which the content in our cups settle and a brew is created — this "brew" is our belief system. We have developed our thought patterns, or beliefs, since we were young. They form our view of the world and ourselves. We are highly influenced by childhood events and our parents, but ultimately it's all about how our minds assign meaning to events.

Same Event, Different Meanings

After becoming a tutor, I have come to realize that children start having negative self-talk much younger than I had previously thought. Some of my primary school students, who are between nine to eleven years old, are already saying things like:

- "I'm stupid."
- "I'm lazy."
- "I'm fat."
- "I'm bad at mathematics."

What's more interesting is that there's another group of students who have a totally different set of beliefs about themselves. When they make mistakes, they joke about it. They say they are just testing me to see if I can spot their mistakes. When they do something right, they are not shy in affirming how clever they are.

Why do similar events mean different things to different children?

Part of it is because of the environment they grew up in. Another factor is that every child has a different way of dealing with and reacting to situations. Some accept what they are told out of obedience; others form beliefs contrary to what they are told out of defiance. Every person, old or young, interprets events differently.

**The same event can mean different things
to different people.**

Even as adults, we give different meanings to the same events. When we make mistakes, some of us think we are useless. But another person might think it's someone else's fault. When our partner has no time for us, some of us might think we are not important to them. But to another person, it might mean they will have more personal time and freedom.

Not all of the meanings we assign to our experiences are true, especially those we assigned during childhood.

Why Do Children Misinterpret Their Experiences?

When we were children, there were many opportunities for us to misinterpret events and believe it meant we were not good enough. You have to understand that the perception of a child and the perception of an adult are different. Right now, in hindsight, it's easy for many of us to understand the intentions of our parents. But, as children, how could we have known our parents cared for us and wanted the best for us? Also, how could we have known they had good intentions but executed them poorly?

Here's an example. Sally thinks her mom loves her sister more than her. She tells herself: *Mommy bought a new bag for my elder sister, but I don't have one. Mommy must love my sister more than me.*

From the mom's perspective, Sally's elder sister is going to start school next year, so she bought her a bag to carry her books. The mom didn't think Sally needed one because she's not starting school yet. It has nothing to do with favoritism. The mom never explained this to Sally, because Sally didn't ask — and Sally never shared what she thought with her parents because she didn't think it mattered. So Sally misinterpreted this event and grew up thinking her mom loved her sister more than her.

Children cannot understand their parents' intentions if they are not shared.

Now, imagine you are a child and your parents had a bad day at work, and they came home exhausted. But the minute they walked into the house, you started asking them questions. You couldn't stop talking about your day at school. You wanted to tell them every single detail. Finally, they lost their patience and asked you to keep quiet. They might have even told you off, unintentionally.

How does this possible scenario make you feel?

Children don't know what's expected of them. If our parents don't explain why they are angry, how can we know they are simply having a bad day? Any criticism directed towards a child can be easily misinterpreted to mean there is something wrong with the child. When our parents lost their cool during times of stress, we might have assumed there was something wrong with us:

- *Was I too noisy?*
- *Maybe my parents don't love me anymore.*

- *Perhaps I'm not important.*
- *I made my parents angry. I must be naughty.*

I used to think my parents didn't love me. I had a difficult time in secondary school, and I wanted to change to a different school. But my parents wouldn't allow me to change. They thought my school was good for me and I should learn how to get along with others better. As an adult, of course, I understand my parents' point of view. Giving up and avoiding something is not the best way to solve an issue. But at the time, no one explained this to me. No one tried to understand what I was going through. I felt powerless and unimportant, and that my parents didn't care about me. This had a huge impact on my self-worth as I was growing up.

Furthermore, even if our parents did share their intentions with us, it doesn't mean we understood it when we were young. Therefore, misunderstandings are bound to happen. Unfortunately, the misinterpretations we develop during childhood can become our deep-seated beliefs for life — until we take action to change them.

How Are Beliefs Formed?

Beliefs are what the mind perceives and accepts to be true. People with low self-esteem don't just view themselves as possibly defective. They are *certain* they are defective.

But is this the truth? No.

Events and their meanings are misinterpreted in the first place, and then our minds keep giving the wrong meaning to similar events, until we firmly believe we just are not good enough and never will be.

My primary school students are not yet fixated on their beliefs. They are still impressionable. If they state the belief that they are stupid — and you tell them they are not and offer a different point of view — they are likely to consider your viewpoint. Unlike teenagers and adults, they are *not* as likely to dismiss ideas contrary to their own. However, once we are adults it's much harder to change our beliefs, especially those held at the unconscious level.

The brain is a system.

It's good at creating habits and automatic responses.

To the mind, it doesn't matter if the meanings assigned to experiences are right or wrong. The brain wants to conserve energy. Once feeling unworthy becomes a habit and part of a person's belief system, it's automatic. You don't need to guess the meaning anymore. It's not: *Maybe my parents didn't love me*, but rather: *I know my parents don't love me*. Also, it's not: *Perhaps I'm not important*, but: *I know I'm not important*.

It's like when we learn how to type. In the beginning, it's very difficult because typing is new to us. We are unsure where all the letters on the keyboard are. So we spend time and attention getting familiar with it. But once we memorize the pattern, we don't have to look at the keyboard anymore. It has become automatic.

Some beliefs are not necessarily real, but once your mind has decided something is true, it feels real to you, no matter what. The mind automatically rejects or filters any contradicting information directed to us going forwards. It doesn't stop and examine each event for what it is anymore. It just keeps producing the same, often-negative feelings and thoughts.

The first three stages of the cup are unavoidable and unconscious for most of us. During these stages, we are too young to understand how the mind works. Also, no matter how positive or caring our parents might have been, they couldn't be there all the time to correct what we thought.

Even if they wanted to, they wouldn't be able to know what we were thinking at every moment. Plus, a few traumatic and emotional incidents in school or at home could be enough to cause limiting self-beliefs for life. So it's almost impossible to stop it from happening.

Eventually, all the negative self-beliefs the mind has created will bring us to the next stage, shaping who we are as a person.

Exercise: Update Your Belief System

Close your eyes and see how you feel about yourself. What feels true for you? Go back to the past and see if there is any incident or situation you might have misinterpreted incorrectly. You might want to clarify what you remember with your parents or anyone else who was involved and their intentions.

Ask yourself: *Are my beliefs still valid for me now? Am I still the unlovable, unimportant child I used to think I was?*

If the answer is "no" to these questions, can you let go of the feelings of unworthiness attached to your outdated beliefs?

Stage 4

IDENTITY

Your first lesson on identity came when you were a toddler. One of the first few things that most parents teach their child is how to say their own name and how to identify "Mommy" and "Daddy."

Initially, toddlers don't realize that the name is referring to them. They don't react to the name you have given them. They might look at you for a second when you call them, but then they go back and play their toys. The child doesn't see themselves as separate from their parents.

But after many repetitions of telling them who they are and seeing themselves in the mirror, they finally realize that this name refers to them and they are separate from their parents. Now, they have an identity: *I am Paul. I am Emily. He is Daddy. She is Mommy.* There's an "I" (who is me) and a "them" (someone who is not me).

Once toddlers understand the concept of identity, they start to create boundaries and more separation. First, they start with their possessions: *This is my toy. This is my pencil. It's not your pencil.* Then, as they grow older, they begin learning to separate themselves by their gender, ethnicity, nationality, and religion. Finally, they form potentially negative beliefs about themselves and people around them:

- *I am not good enough.*
- *I am not worthy of love.*
- *They don't love me.*
- *I need to do this to get their attention.*
- *If I don't obey my parents, they will get angry.*

These negative self-beliefs wouldn't have existed in the first place if we didn't have an identity. For the rest of our life, we continue to build our identity with the work we do, our relationships with others, and what we love. We spend time figuring out and establishing who we are, and who we are not.

Self-beliefs can only be formed

when there is an identity and a concept of separation.

The Fourth Stage of the cup is about building and protecting identity. Even though we have an identity before our self-beliefs are formed, I have placed identity after the "beliefs" stage because identity is not completely established during our early years. There is still room for change. Even when we become teenagers, for the most part, our sense of self is still somewhat confused. Identity is made up of beliefs and the evidence that supports these beliefs, but this process is not solidified until we become older.

Unlike the third stage, once our identity has been more or less established, it has a stronger grip on us. Individual beliefs can be changed with the right resources and new perspectives. But for identity, we tend to hold onto and protect it dearly.

The Need to Protect Our Identity

Have you ever rejected compliments? Ask yourself why. Logically speaking, everyone loves to be praised. Why do you feel so uncomfortable being praised?

As someone who has low self-esteem, I noticed that every time someone gave me a compliment, I would start to squirm and cringe. I didn't know how to handle compliments and I felt really awkward. At the back of my mind, I used to think that people were either being polite or being insincere. Upon reflection, I realized I felt uncomfortable because I couldn't identify with what they were saying. It didn't fit with the self-image my mind had created for me.

If you have believed you are not good enough for a long time, and someone praises you, doesn't it oppose what you believe about yourself? They are basically telling you the identity you have created for yourself all this time is wrong. This is not going to sit too well with your mind. Subconsciously, we have a tendency to defend and protect our low self-esteem identity even if it doesn't do us any good.

Identity is created by the mind
and for the mind.

At the Fourth Stage of the cup, the mind becomes focused on ego. The cup is no longer just a cup. We perceive the cup and its content to be us, our self-image. There is no separation between who we are and the mental image of self created by our minds.

Our minds have decided who we are, and who we are not, and we wholeheartedly believe in this incorrect identity. Unlike the previous two stages, you don't let anyone pour things into your cup without your permission. This is the stage at which we protect the cup and its content. We refuse to let people who have beliefs contrary to ours near our cup. We only let those whose beliefs resonate with us pour content into our cup. No one is allowed to spoil the brew our minds have created for us.

For those with low self-esteem, this is a vicious cycle. When your cup is filled with negative beliefs about yourself, you only resonate with events that support these negative beliefs. If people say you are clever, you don't believe them, because being clever has never been part of your identity. On the other hand, if you make a mistake, you are likely to quickly identify yourself as dumb without any hesitation, even though you are intelligent. You constantly seek evidence that supports your identity to make your identity stronger, and you disregard any information that isn't part of your identity.

In other words, our beliefs shape our identity — and our identity keeps our beliefs intact. They work hand in hand. So people who have high self-esteem continue to feel good about themselves, while people with low self-esteem will continue to feel worse. The more we protect our identity, the stronger it gets.

But why don't we just get rid of our low self-esteem identity?

Why Is It So Hard to Let Go of Our Identity?

Letting go of our identity is not easy. We are attached to it because it gives us a sense of self-importance. Our identity has been with us for years. What will remain when we let go of everything we know about ourselves? Who will we be? How will we be able to function?

As mentioned in Chapter 1, the mind is afraid of being emptied. It is made up of automatic systems and habits. This helps the mind conserve energy. Once we let go of our low self-esteem identity, the mind will have to start all over again, collecting new information about us and building a new identity.

You can't change the outside without changing the inside.

Furthermore, there are two types of identity. One is the outer identity; the other is the inner identity. The outer identity is the one you present to other people. It's what people know you as. The inner identity, on the other hand, is what you identify yourself with and what you believe about yourself. Others can't see it. But unlike the outer identity, it's not tangible. It's inside your mind, so you might not even be aware you have low self-esteem.

Most of us try to build our outer identity, hoping we will feel better about ourselves. But it's the inner identity residing in our subconscious that makes us feel inferior. This is why people with low self-esteem are often misunderstood. Our outer identity and inner identity might contradict each other. We might be a Ph.D. (outer identity), but we identify ourselves as being stupid (inner identity). Even if we are fashion models (outer identity), we can still feel ugly inside (inner identity). Others can only perceive our outer identity, so they never understand how we feel or perceive ourselves to be.

Lastly, even if we are aware of our inner identity, we might not know how to change it, or we might think change is impossible. We might not be aware that our identity has been created by past conditioning, false beliefs, and misinterpretations from our childhood. To us, it is simply who we are, something we thought we were given at birth. Not everyone with low self-esteem thinks of changing it, at least not initially, when low self-esteem is still bearable.

When Do We Leave This Stage?

Everyone goes through the first four stages, but not everyone will move on to the next stage. People stay in this stage because they are unaware of the previous stages. They don't know how the mind works and they accept their low self-esteem identity. They believe every thought they have is absolute truth, and they never question them.

Also, if someone's mind has built a somewhat positive identity, they probably won't see a need to change. If their mind keeps telling them they are the best — even when they have some problems and issues in life — they will blame others or the world for their misfortune. They will choose to protect their positive self-image instead of changing it, because there's little incentive for them to change.

However, if you are like me and your mind has built a negative self-image, then you are likely motivated to change your identity. I was so tortured by my constant negative thoughts and painful emotions that I had no choice but to take action.

When the brew in your cup becomes unbearable, you will have no choice but to change it.

That day, when I had a meltdown in the toilet cubicle, there were two paths I could have taken. One was to remain as a victim and continue to suffer; the other was to change and grow. I chose the latter because I didn't want to suffer anymore. Imagine not feeling good about yourself all the time, and no matter what you or anyone else does your mind tells you that it's your fault and *you* are the problem. It's miserable to live with a mind like this. So I could see no other way but to change.

Your mind will move on to the next stage once you

have decided to change. My mind started to lose control over me because my decision was, basically, to tell it that I was no longer willing to suffer with low self-esteem.

When you make the decision to let go of the negative parts of your identity, you will begin to find resources and people around you that will help you. It's like driving on a road. You will miss the pleasant sights if you are totally focused on reaching your destination, but once you start looking for a gas station, you will find one.

That's how I found the resources I needed to help me change my negative beliefs about myself.

Exercise: Accept Compliments

Think of the times when people praised you. How did it make you feel? Did you turn down their compliments and downplay your success? Did you credit your success to luck or someone else? Did you return the favor by complimenting them immediately, or did you doubt their sincerity?

Learn to accept compliments. The next time someone praises you, say "thank you" and be grateful. Notice what your mind tells you. It might say something like: *I don't deserve this, or I'm so full of myself.* Realize this is the identity your mind created for you. You don't have to *do* anything to stop these thoughts. *Awareness* of how the mind works will eventually wear down its grip on you. It's all about learning to pay attention.

Stage 5

JUDGE

Up to this point, our subconscious mind has been running our lives. Studies have shown that 95 percent of our behaviors and reactions happen at the subconscious level. Our subconscious stores memories, forms beliefs, and creates our identity. It operates efficiently by developing habits and automating what we do. However, these habits and beliefs can cause us to suffer because they are based on past conditioning that is untrue or outdated.

Once we decide to change our identity, our conscious

mind takes over and we move to the next stage of the cup — the judging stage.

Our conscious mind judges what is good and bad for us.

The Fifth Stage is all about making judgments. Our *conscious* mind decides what thoughts, beliefs, habits, and behaviors are best for us. We become extra careful and selective about what goes into our cup. Similar to the fourth stage, we protect the cup from external sources. But the difference is that this time we judge what is right for us, instead of letting in negative content automatically because it resonates with our *subconscious* beliefs. We can use a "spoon" to remove the content in the cup that is making the brew taste bad and enhance the taste by introducing new content.

At this stage, you might also realize your subconscious mind is changing the way it talks to you. Instead of having thoughts such as: *I am stupid, I'm not good enough,* and *I'm ugly,* the thoughts now become: *You are stupid, You are not good enough,* and *You are ugly.* This means your consciousness has disassociated from your subconscious, and you no longer see yourself the way your subconscious created for you. You no longer believe everything your subconscious says. There is a space between you and your subconscious. You will know you are making good progress when the critical voice inside your head changes from *I am* to *You are*.

But this stage has its own set of problems, too. Even though we suffer less when we detach ourselves from our subconscious mind, the nagging, critical voice is still there. Instead of feeling bad about ourselves, now we have an enemy we want to get rid of called "the inner critic." Our past conditioning and negative thought patterns are so deeply ingrained in our subconscious, they can't be changed or removed overnight without the help of techniques and strategies such as:

- Affirmations
- The Law of Attraction
- Positive thinking
- Hypnosis
- EFT (Emotional Freedom Technique), and
- NLP (Neuro-Linguistic Programming)

Furthermore, as we start to challenge our subconscious and change our beliefs, we also open "Pandora's Box." Even though our self-esteem might improve and the critical voice in our head might quiet down, the inner critic is not the only voice inside our head. Once our main identity starts to wear down, the other voices in our subconscious (also known as subpersonalities in psychology) begin to get louder.

The Never-Ending Conflict

There is this hilarious scene from Disney's animated features, Tangled, where the main character, Rapunzel, is having an internal conflict. One moment, she is so excited and happy that she stepped out of the tower for the first time. Another moment, she is cowering in fear and guilt because she has disobeyed her mom. The next scene, we see her running around and kicking the leaves with joy. Then, she feels guilty again for being a horrible daughter. She keeps switching between happiness and guilt, until Flynn, the main male character, stops her. Even though this is a scene from a movie, and the internal conflict Rapunzel experiences is exaggerated, it's something we can all relate to.

You've probably had the experience of hearing more than one voice in your head, too. It is as though we are characters in a cartoon or comic strip, making a tough decision. An angel and a devil appear on each of our shoulders, whispering things into our ears and giving us suggestions. Sometimes, they are helpful; other times they are not. But one thing's for sure; these voices are always debating and at odds with each other, causing inner turmoil in us. This is the work of our subpersonalities.

If you don't notice this for yourself, observe it in other people. Sometimes, people can be cheerful and friendly one day, but when you see them again a few days later they are angry and unpleasant to be with. There's an idiom for this, "Getting up on the wrong side of the bed." How about when someone genuinely promises you they will never do something again? A few days later, the unknowing promise is broken. The spiritual teacher Eckhart Tolle said in one of his seminars that this scenario is the result of "different personalities emerging at different times."

**Our internal conflict is caused by
the different subpersonalities we hold.**

Initially, we thought we could take a spoon and remove the negative beliefs in our cup, one by one. Little do we know that underneath these negative beliefs, there is a wide array of other beliefs that have accumulated in our subconscious over our lifetime. We don't just have one identity; we have many identities. So we have removed the beliefs related to low self-esteem and unworthiness. But these are not the only beliefs stored in our subconscious. How about the others?

During childhood, we formed many beliefs related to money, relationships, work, life, and more. Beliefs of a similar nature and worldviews are grouped together to create parts of our total identity. They are neither good nor bad, but they have different opinions and get into conflict with one another easily.

For example, you might have a workaholic identity that causes you to value work and achievement. It tells you: *You need to get this done today.* But you might also have a child identity that encourages you to take a break and play: *You have already worked so hard for the past week. It's the weekend. Take a break instead.*

Which "voice" is right? It's up to your conscious mind to judge and decide.

Let's say you eventually give in to your child identity and take a break. After the break, you realize that your work is nowhere near completion. Now, your inner critic steps in and gives you a scolding: *You should have done your work. Now, you'll never meet your deadline.* This voice makes you feel guilty.

This is just one example how our subpersonalities create conflict. Other common examples include:

- Wanting to watch television versus wanting to exercise
- Wanting to stay healthy versus wanting to snack
- Wanting to be spontaneous versus wanting to have every detail planned
- Wanting to be wealthy versus wanting to be comfortable, and
- Wanting to grow and change versus wanting to stay the same

When we are in Stage 4, even though we don't like ourselves, it's relatively easier to make decisions.

Everything is habitual and decided by our subconscious. But at Stage 5, our conscious mind decides what's best for us. It faces tremendous stress in making the right decisions. Like the shoulder and devil angels, every subpersonality is asking the conscious mind to listen to it. This creates problems and confusion for the conscious mind and increases its workload. It is so used to operating at five percent of the brain activity. Now, it has to use more energy to resolve these issues.

Ultimately, this never-ending conflict among our subpersonalities causes us to over-think everything, leaving us feeling stuck, stressed, and overwhelmed, even though we feel more worthy of ourselves now.

Why Doesn't Judging Help Eventually?

In 2009, I enrolled in my first online program ever, *Morty Lefkoe's Natural Confidence*. Not only did it help me get rid of 23 common beliefs and conditioning, it changed my life completely. My negative self-talk diminished tremendously , just by doing this one course. I used the same technique to remove many of my limiting beliefs and my self-esteem improved tremendously. It was the first, major turning point of my life.

Over the next six years, I participated in programs with other experts, too. I introduced new beliefs about myself and developed a more positive mindset. Even though I had some internal conflicts once in awhile, my life was still stable and enjoyable, for the most part.

But it wasn't until I had depression at the end of 2015 that I realized my low self-esteem identity didn't die; it just took a backseat. With the right trigger, it's capable of unleashing its full power and control over me. This made me wonder: *Does replacing old beliefs with new, positive ones work at all? Can we be happy and peaceful just by changing our beliefs, or it is just a temporary solution?*

Even though I'm grateful for the six years of bliss the online programs gave me, I realize changing closely held beliefs is not entirely effective in the long run. Here's why.

1. We don't know how much depth there is to our subconscious mind.

The mind is a complex mechanism. Many types of research have been done on the human mind, but there are still many things we don't know about it. We don't know how much is stored in the mind and how to access it easily. It's not like a filing cabinet that we can see and go through the files one-by-one.

The beliefs we thought we had removed
might just be archived.

No matter how detailed we are in cleaning up our subconscious mind, there will be some negative beliefs that slip through the cracks. We also can't tell whether the negative beliefs are removed completely. Some events might not trigger our beliefs anymore, but we don't know if others triggers exist until they activate our sense of unworthiness.

2. Our conscious mind can only do so much.

Ideally, we want to use our conscious mind to change our subconscious mind so it will do our bidding. But, in reality, it's very taxing for the conscious mind to do this.

You can't guard the cup 24/7.

As mentioned previously, we only use our conscious mind five percent of the time. We have the tendency to rely on our subconscious mind for many things, because it's easy and energy saving to just let it go on autopilot. The conscious mind can't possibly judge all the new information that comes in. It's too much work for the conscious mind and we are bound to make mistakes. Often, we don't realize we have fallen back to the subconscious level until it's too late.

In addition, if we are perfectionist about it and get frustrated, we might end up blaming and beating ourselves up for making mistakes. This gives our inner critic the chance to grow stronger.

3. Judging shuts off some of the subpersonalities.

Judging requires our conscious mind to make conclusions. It has to decide what is right and what is wrong. Every time it supports a subpersonality, it is also ignoring another subpersonality, another "voice," at the same time. Gradually, our conscious mind develops its preferences. It favors one subpersonality over another. For the ease of judging, our conscious mind is likely to suppress a few subpersonalities that are deemed harmful to us, or not part of the new identity we are building.

Take, for instance, the previous example on working hard. After being shamed by the inner critic numerous times for not completing work on time, our conscious mind might decide to ignore the child identity completely. Seeing the child identity as the main source of conflict, we don't listen to the child identity and its suggestions anymore. However, this might not be a good thing in the long run, because we can end up working too hard and not taking breaks when necessary, causing us to feel exhausted and overwhelmed.

All subpersonalities serve a purpose.

On the flip side, if we decide to shut off our inner critic and let our child identity be in control all the time, we can end up having too much fun, not meeting deadlines, and getting ourselves into trouble.

Each subpersonality has its merits. By being overly judgmental, we run the risk of discrediting the value of our other subpersonalities.

4. It's impossible to separate the good from the bad.

Most of us would rather have positive beliefs than negative beliefs. But how do we tell whether a belief is positive or not?

I am confident. Is this a positive belief or a negative one? Being confident before giving a public presentation can calm down your nerves and help you deliver your speech the best you can. But being confident can also result in under-preparation for your presentation. On the contrary, believing that you are not confident might actually urge you to prepare and rehearse more.

So is: *I can do it a good belief?* It does seem better than: *I can't do it.* At least it gets you into action. But what if you really can't do something you believe you can do? Are you going to be disappointed by your high expectations or over-promise someone something you can't deliver? Being optimistic doesn't mean everything will always work out.

We don't always know if a belief

is good for us, or not.

What we think is bad

might actually be beneficial.

The truth is beliefs are neither positive nor negative. The so-called negative beliefs get us to change and grow. They serve a purpose, too. It all depends on how an individual perceives and uses each belief to their advantage.

The mind cannot predict the future. We don't know if something will *eventually* be good for us, or not. Our conscious mind merely provides a judgment, an opinion, not necessarily the truth. So we might be adding the wrong content to the cup thinking it's good for us.

5. The conscious mind relies on the subconscious mind to judge.

How does our conscious mind judge what is right or wrong for us? It relies a lot on our past experiences and preconceived beliefs to infer what is appropriate. But isn't this going back to consulting our subconscious?

What we take out of our cups depends on
what we have in them.

Most of the time, our judgments are based on what we already have in our subconscious mind. We do it so subtly that we might not even be aware of it. When new information comes into our awareness, the mind immediately taps into the large database inside our subconscious and looks for similar patterns and experiences. This is habitual. Even though our conscious mind tries to judge each situation as it is, we are highly influenced by the subconscious.

When we perceive the inner critic as an enemy, it's because our past experiences with self-criticism reminds us how inferior we used to feel. Our inner critic triggers our lack of self-worth, and we don't want to experience that feeling again. For someone who hasn't experience low self-esteem before, or doesn't identify with it, the inner critic doesn't hurt them at all. In fact, they think it's necessary for self-discipline.

6. Judging isn't solving the core problem.

What do most people do when they have a problem? They look at the cause of the problem and try to fix it. When we know our negative self-beliefs are causing us to feel unworthy, we try to fix and replace them with better self-beliefs. But judging the content in the cup and removing the undesirable parts from the cup doesn't help us love ourselves.

Whenever we judge ourselves, we are also evaluating our worthiness and forming opinions about ourselves in the process. The mere act of judging is already telling ourselves that there's part of us that is good, and part of us that is not good. How do we love ourselves unconditionally when we can't accept all of who we are?

Furthermore, the mind is just building another identity for us to base our self-esteem on. If reality and our new beliefs align, that's great. But what if they don't align; what happen to our self-worth then? The problem is never about our self-beliefs or the negative thoughts and emotions they produce.

The problem is we associate our sense of self with these beliefs.

We are still attached to the cup and its content. The content in the cup is still our focus, and it continues to affect how we perceive our self-worth, even though the content in the cup has been changed to something more positive.

A Positive Identity Is Still an Identity

In the fourth episode of *Survivor: Kaôh Rōng*, three castaways collapsed after suffering from heatstroke and exhaustion while participating in one of the reward challenges. Caleb Reynolds, one of the three castaways, was medically evacuated from the game after his heart rate continued to drop. Digging the sandpit under the grueling heat was brutal. But if they had not first identified themselves as tough and competitive to the show producers, would they have collapsed? After all, they were just competing for coffee and spices. Why did they push themselves so hard?

A positive self-image is a trap, too.

All aspects of our identity, whether positive or negative, are still mind-made. The subconscious has created them based on our beliefs, and beliefs are only opinions about what we think is true. They are not necessarily the truth. As long as we are identified with the image the mind has produced, we are still controlled by our mind.

Another castaway, Debbie Wanner, described her heatstroke experience in one of her confessions, "Even when I was feeling utterly on the brink of collapse, my mind was saying: *Winners don't quit. Pain is weakness leaving the body.*" Debbie knew she was going to collapse, but she still listened to what her mind told her to do. Even when the challenge was over for their tribe, she refused to ask for help because she didn't want to appear weak. She has always prided herself on taking care of herself and her family and being strong.

The same goes for the other two collapsed castaways. Caleb said in one of his interviews that he had so much adrenaline going that he couldn't stop. Cydney Gillon was described as a machine that doesn't have an "off" switch button by another castaway. Where did the "off" button to their mind go?

Their positive images of themselves prevented them from seeing the truth and the situation for what it was. If they had more awareness, they would have listened to their bodies and known it's not okay to push them any further. But instead they felt a need to protect and uphold their self-image of being strong, and give control to their mind.

Even though the following identities are positive, they make us act the way the mind wants us to act:

- I am successful.
- I am nice.
- I am spiritual.
- I am generous.

- I am smart.

The mind creates tunnel vision. When we are so focused on maintaining our positive identity, we lose track of who we really are. We only see what the mind wants us to be. It's like focusing on a ball that rolls onto the road. We are so focused on getting the ball that we don't notice the oncoming traffic, which can be dangerous.

We don't love ourselves.

We just love the image our mind has created for us.

Kristin Neff, the author of *Self-Compassion*, encourages us to opt out on the self-esteem game. Rather than constantly evaluating how good or worthy we are, why not get our worthiness out of the picture and love ourselves just as we are?

Identity, worthiness, and self-esteem are nothing other than mental games and concepts created by the mind. The mind loves to judge and compare, and it will continue to do so. There's no end to it. Once we achieve the identity the mind has created for us, it compares us with other people and then creates a "better" identity for us to pursue.

What comes out of this comparison is only a continual feeling of not being good enough. So never let your mind define who you are.

In the next chapter, we will see what happens if the identity created for us has fallen apart.

Exercise: Become Aware of Your Internal Conflicts

The next time you experience an internal conflict, stop and notice your thoughts. Your task is not to stop, interfere, or change those thoughts. Your task is just to listen to them and be a neutral observer. Write down what you observe after the conflict ends.

Ask yourself: *What triggers this internal conflict?* Without judging the thoughts, can you see that both points of views are valid in different contexts? Also, notice your tendency to judge and shut out one point of view.

Stage 6

AWAKENING

I was watching an interview one day on the local news. The host was interviewing an ex-drug addict, who is now helping to counsel other drug addicts. The host asked him, "What made you decide to quit drugs?"

"One day, I looked in the mirror at my reflection for a good 15 minutes," said the ex-addict. "I just could not recognize myself anymore. My eyes were sunken. There wasn't any glow in my face. That day, I realized what drugs had done to me."

This is exactly how it felt like to be awakened, I thought to myself.

When you don't know who you are anymore,
consider it an opportunity for awakening.

When I interviewed Larry Jacobson for my first book, *Fearless Passion*, I didn't quite get his fear about letting go of his identity. I understood intellectually that he was giving up his career and income to sail around the world. That's huge. But emotionally, I didn't feel the impact of his losing his usual identity. It wasn't until I lost my own identity as an animator that I realized how dearly I was holding onto my work to give my life meaning.

After being an animator for three months, I realized that animation was not for me, but I didn't want to go back to being an accountant again. Not only was accounting too much of a boring routine, I had just published a book that encourages people to pursue their dreams and passion. I had told everyone I was switching to the animation industry. How could I go back to being an accountant again? Suddenly, I was nobody. I had no direction. I was lost. I didn't know what to do with my life.

As I mentioned before, each subpersonality has a purpose. I thought I had gotten rid of my low self-esteem six years before, but it was back. It had never left. It was just hiding in a corner waiting to be called forth. During the period of no identity, I was numb to my emotions of shame, worthlessness, and fear, pretending that everything was fine. But then, my inner critic came back to belittle me and urge me to feel the pain, because suppressing pain isn't good for the body. For the next two months, I sank into deep depression.

But who would have thought that depression could change a person's life?

One day, I was at the river contemplating jumping in. A part of me was suffering from the pain; another part of me said jump in and end the pain. There was yet another part of me that was scared I might actually jump into the river. I froze, unsure what to do next, so I took a seat on one of the benches.

As I was sitting there looking at the trees and the sky, I gradually slipped into a state of total peace. There was no noise in my head. I was just enjoying the beauty of nature that surrounded me. Just being in nature had taken me out of the drama of my mind without any conscious effort on my part.

After some time, another voice came and offered me new meaning and purpose. This voice told me to write my experience into a book and share it with other people who have depression. This time, the voice was so loud and firm that it drowned out all the other voices. I was completely healed of my depression from that point forwards.

When you are in a dream,

it takes a nightmare to wake you up.

Losing my identity eventually became my key to spiritual awakening. After that incident, I started wondering who the real me was. I hadn't recognized who I was for two months. I was so unlike "me." Why were there conflicting voices in my head? Why was there a "me" who wanted to die, and another "me" who wanted to live? Which one was the real "me"? It was like waking up from a bad nightmare.

With the help of spiritual books, I finally realized I'm not the mind. I was performing mindfulness that day at the river without even realizing that's what it was.

This is the Sixth Stage of the cup, the stage of spiritual awakening. It's when we realize we are not our thoughts, beliefs, or emotions — not just from a conceptual level, but from a deeper level of knowingness.

Unfortunately, not everyone gets awakened when they lose their identity.

When the Cup Topples

When we think our life is getting better, something challenging hits us and knocks over our cup. All the mental content we have been protecting over the years is now spilled all over the place. Our identity has been destroyed. The beliefs we hold on to so dearly are no longer true for us. Everything we believe can make us feel good has been ruined.

What do we do then?

Life challenges are not that uncommon. Examples include:

- Having a serious accident on the road
- Losing a job
- Losing someone in our family
- Ending of a relationship, and
- Having a life-threatening disease

These life situations can cause us to lose our identity, one way or another. The size and severity of the life challenge doesn't matter. But it does matter what we do after our cups have been knocked over. Here are three possible choices:

1. We cry over spilled milk.

This is exactly how I reacted for two months when my cup got knocked over. Instead of picking my cup up, I was crying over the loss of my identity. The animator identity, which I had taken three years to build, was gone within a few months and I couldn't accept it.

This is probably the most common response of the three. Even if it's just for a short period of time, we usually start by reacting or feeling some form of non-acceptance towards the situation. Some of us panic: *What should I do now?* Some of us regret our past actions: *If only I have taken better care of my body, I wouldn't have this disease.* Some of us experience shock: *I can't believe this is happening to me.* Non-acceptance eventually leads us to become a victim of circumstances.

When we chose this response, we look exactly like a toppled cup. We lie down and feel hopeless and depressed.

Nothing seems to work for us.

But what are we crying for?

We cry for the loss of our identity.

The content spilled is part of who we think we are.

When we lose our parents, we cry because they are no longer with us, or are we crying for the loss of our childhood identity? When we become bankrupt, are we crying for the loss of money, or are we crying for the loss of our identity as a rich person? When we have a life-threatening disease, are we crying because we are going to die, or are we crying for the loss of our identity as a healthy, able-bodied person?

It could be both. Whenever we face a life challenge, a part of us will grieve the loss of our identity. Identities are not eternal. We have difficulty accepting it when we have to give up one of our identities.

2. We pick up the cup and start over again.

Eventually, some of us who have suffered enough choose to pick ourselves up again and start over. We pick up the toppled cup, collect whatever is still remaining in the cup, and refill the cup. We rebuild our identity, find solutions to our problems, and become hopeful again. We don't know why we had to face a particular challenge, but we are glad it's over. We get on with our life; some of us might even forget how vulnerable we were as we faced our difficulties.

When we choose this response, we go back to being the judge again, the Fifth Stage of the cup. The mind is back in control. This is fine until another life challenge comes and topples the cup again, and we become upset and cry again. Thus, the cycle can only keep repeating itself.

Life won't stop challenging us, because life doesn't see difficult events as challenges. We all experience deaths, deterioration of the physical body, loss of a loved one, and loss of our identities.

We know on a deeper level that the physical body will be gone, one day. Yet, mentally we have trouble accepting this truth. We try to hang onto a self-image that once was, without acknowledging we will perish one day. Each life challenge is actually an opportunity for reflection and awakening, a chance for us to see the truth. It isn't the suffering the mind makes it out to be.

3. We realize we are not the cup.

There are two ways to become awakened. The first is to realize we have been solving the wrong problem all along. The problem isn't with our beliefs; it's our attachment to our mind-made identity. This awareness could come from spiritual books, resources, or teachers, including this one I'm writing. We start to explore who we really are and eventually we get awakened.

But this is hardly the case for most people. Most of us don't pick up spiritual books until something painful happens.

Suffering helps us change.

The only way to survive suffering is to grow.

The second way to spiritual awakening is through direct experience with suffering, which is the best spiritual teacher. When our minds cause us to suffer a great deal, we have no choice but to change. There is nothing to lose when we are at rock bottom. Isn't this how most of us progressed from Stage 4 to Stage 5? The Universe doesn't give us anything we can't handle. If we are given a challenge, it means we are ready to be awakened. The toppled cup is our chance to find out who we really are and create a more positive life experience.

When your cup is toppled and its content spilled out, do you realize you are still here? Can you feel your heart beating and your lungs breathing? Isn't this life? Isn't this who you are? You are looking at the toppled cup. You are the hand that picks up the cup. The only time you will suffer is when you accept the toppled cup as your identity.

We are not the cup and its content. Your cup might be emptied, but it doesn't take away the aliveness that you are. When you were a baby, wasn't your cup always empty, and yet you were still alive? Once you became aware that your cup could be emptied, it no longer mattered how many times it was knocked over. It doesn't affect who you are, because you can always pick up your cup again.

With this kind of awareness, the mind loses its power over us.

Who Am I?

My first epiphany came when I was reading Eckhart Tolle's The Power of Now. In his introduction, he shares that once he had a peculiar thought: I cannot live with myself any longer. He goes on to explain his realization:

Am I one or two?
If I cannot live with myself, there must be two of me:
the 'I' and the 'self' that 'I' cannot live with.
Maybe only one of them is real.

I immediately understood what he meant, because I had the same experience when I was at the river. I realized the real "me," my spiritual self, observes the thinker. It watches the visual images my mind produces, and listens to the noises my mind makes. I know I am not the mind.

I'm the observer.

Looking back at the incident I experienced by the river, I have new insights about my true identity. The "me" who suffered from the pain was just part of the victim identity my mind had created. The "me" who was so relentlessly critical during those two months is the inner critic. The "me" who instigated the idea of my jumping in the water was protecting me from feeling the pain. Even the "me" who told me not to jump was one of my subpersonalities, and it was afraid to die.

However, all of them are not the real me. They are

just identities and subpersonalities created by my subconscious mind from my past conditioning and mental preferences. The real me simply observes the beauty of nature. I was in touch with the real me during that short period of time when I had no thoughts, just sense perceptions. My cup was empty. I wasn't even paying attention to the cup.

I am the calm, quiet, and peaceful spiritual being that is always here, always present. When I'm in touch with my true self in this way, it allows the most appropriate voice to be heard and guide me to the next action.

To help you understand this concept, here is another analogy.

The Movie Analogy

When I was in Bali for an entrepreneur program, our mentor, Roger Hamilton, told us that there are three of him — The Audience Roger, The Director Roger, and The Actor Roger.

1. The Audience: He watches the movie and is detached from it. He's the observer. All he wants is a movie that is worth watching. He knows things

will get better for the actor, eventually.

2. The Director: He makes a movie that is worth watching. He writes the script for the actor and tells him what to do.

3. The Actor: He does the work. He's like a character in the movie. He doesn't know what will happen next, or that circumstances will improve.

At that time, I couldn't fully understand his analogy, especially when he started talking about Hindu deities. I wondered what he meant when he said there's a part of us (the audience) who is just watching as everything unfolds.

We are not in the movie.

We are just watching the movie.

After I had the direct experience with my spiritual self, I finally understood what Roger Hamilton meant. Our spiritual self is like an audience watching a movie. We are not in the movie. But sometimes when we watch a movie, we are so absorbed in the movie that we forget we are not actually *in* the movie. In these moments, we suffer along with the actor and feel their pain and emotions, not realizing we are just the audience, not the actor. This is what spiritual teachers refer to as "being unconscious."

The mind is like a director who tells an actor what to do — the actor is like our bodies carrying out the instructions given by the director. The director gives the actor a role to play, just like our minds give our bodies an identity to uphold.

As the audience, we don't get to choose what movie the director makes, but we can choose not to watch the movie. Movies are made for the audience, not for the director. A movie that isn't worth watching loses the attention of its audience. Similarly, if we don't give our attention to the identity created by the mind, it doesn't have any power or effect on us. If we are not interested in what the mind has to say, we can always choose not to listen to it. We can just observe and empty our thoughts as they come. This is what spirituality teachers, Buddhists, therapists, and psychologists mean by "mindfulness."

Furthermore, when we are aware that the movie and we are separate entities, our problem becomes small and manageable because we are detached from it and looking at it at a distance. But if we look at our problem as though we are the actor, then the problem becomes huge, because we are inside the problem and trying to get out.

Movies will end eventually,
just like suffering doesn't last forever.

Conflict is only good for the duration of the movie. The human mind and body have an expiration date, too. We, the audience, will ultimately leave the cinema and return to daily life. We can't stay in the cinema forever, no matter how dramatic or interesting a movie is. Dr. Wayne Dyer, a spiritual teacher, describes it best in his books. He says we are just "tourists on Earth." One day, we have to return to the Source that created us. Everything we experience as physical form is just temporary. We can't take it with us once we leave the world.

But we don't have to wait till the movie ends to realize we are the audience. The audience has a life beyond the movie, and we can leave the movie before it ends. Plus, most of our suffering is just a rerun of our past memories. It isn't worth our time to watch them so much.

Awakening Is Awareness and Experience

If you've read up to this point and you don't get what spiritual awakening is all about, that's okay. You don't have to believe that you are the spirit. Spirituality is neither a belief nor a concept. It cannot be grasped by your mind because it is not something created by your mind. You'll have to experience it yourself to know it.

**Spiritual awakening is
a direct experience of the truth.**

Similar to what William Shakespeare wrote in *Romeo and Juliet*, "A rose by any other name would smell as sweet," it doesn't matter if you call yourself "the spirit," or not. You can call yourself whatever you want to. My psychologist friend told me about the sky analogy, which is used in the field of psychology. The awareness is the sky, and the changing weather represents our thoughts and feelings. Our thoughts and feelings come and go at different intervals, but the sky always remains. The psychologist called this "awareness." Spiritual teachers speak of the spirit. Both are fine, because the name doesn't take away the essence of the truth.

As long as you are aware and have a direct experience that you are the one behind the mind (observing all the drama the mind creates) you are awakened. The mind can present you with different ideas, thoughts, and emotions to get you to do something, but only you can make the final decision. You are awake when you *know* you have the power to choose which thoughts to listen to, or not listen to.

In order to awaken, your direct experience with the truth needs awareness. Even though some of us meditate daily, we don't always find much peace outside of meditation, because we meditate without the awareness of who we are. Meditation to us is just a ritual to slow down or stop our thoughts. We use it to shut off and escape the mind. It's no different that being addicted to food, drugs, sex, or television. In essence, we still identify ourselves with the mind.

It's not about becoming;
it's about being.

There's nothing wrong with scheduling a fixed time each day to meditate. But we are not trying to become more peaceful through meditation, because we already are the peace. The observer is always neutral and peaceful. Meditation is just one way to help us connect to who we already are.

Peace is always present throughout the day. The only difference lies between whether we are aware of it, or not. Having a fixed meditation routine can remind us of who we are, but it's not necessary. Many moments during the day, we can be mindful of who we are and feel the peace, regardless of what we are doing.

Exercise: Record Your Experience

What is your direct experience of spirit? How does it feel to be awakened and in touch with being the observer? How is it different when you are identified with your mind? Write down your experience and observation. It might be difficult to record in words. If that's the case, remember the feeling instead.

Also, notice how your mind tries to make sense of your experience, but can't. Let go of your mind's need to understand everything. Trust your innate knowingness. Recognize that if the movie your mind is playing isn't something worth watching, you can always direct your attention somewhere else. You don't have to complete a movie that doesn't serve your best interests.

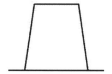

Stage 7

MASTERY

After we have awakened, what's next? Most of us don't stay awake after our initial experience. Even though we know we are spirit, and not the mind, we still value the mind over the spirit. It's shown in our common language. People usually say, "mind, body, and spirit." They don't say, "spirit, body, and mind." The word "mind" always comes first.

Moreover, the mind has more control over us than we realize. We know we are not our thoughts, but do we know it every single moment? When we forget, we fall asleep. In spirituality, this is called "being unconscious." As we carry on with our daily life, it's easy to lose our awareness and let the mind remain in control.

We forget we are the master and

the cup is only our tool.

One day in May 2013, I sat on the steps of TKTS Times Square, shivering in the cold for a good 45 minutes. What was I doing there? I was undecided as to which Broadway show to attend.

My initial inclination was to watch the Broadway play *Orphans*. But somehow, my mind wasn't convinced. It started listing reasons why I shouldn't watch this particular play and why I should watch a musical, instead. It babbled nonstop, reminding me how bad my English was and saying it was a waste of money, because I wouldn't be able to comprehend it.

It's true. Sometimes, it's challenging for me to watch movies in English without the subtitles. However, I wasn't going to let my mind stop me from enjoying a play in New York. So I decided to outwit the mind at its own game; I decided to use reasoning. I thought of all the reasons why watching the play was a good idea and tried to convince my mind to *let* me watch the play.

Ultimately, I won. I convinced my mind.

But to what end? I had spent 45 minutes in the cold, feeling miserable.

In retrospect, this seems laughable, especially now that I know how the mind works. My subconscious created the conflict in the first place, and my conscious mind fell into the trap when it tried to resolve the problem by defending my choice. I had made myself powerless by following the endless stream of thoughts between the two.

At the same time, this is unbelievable. What was I doing? Why did I allow myself to sit out in the cold for so long? I already knew I wanted to watch *Orphans*. Why did I need to convince my mind and ask for permission to do something? When did my mind gain so much power over me?

When did it become my master?

Who Is the Master?

Apart from knowing we are not the mind, we need to know we are the *masters* of the mind, not the other way around.

The last stage of the cup is about mastery and learning how to keep our cups empty. What do we do with the toppled cup? Do we throw it away? Leave it lying down? If we put the cup straight up again, the cup might get filled up without our noticing. If we block it from getting filled up, perhaps we are paying too much attention to it. So how do we keep the cup empty forever?

The answer is we don't. We don't keep our cups empty all the time. The mind can't stay empty forever. It has been programmed to get filled up; it was meant to be used. For practical reasons, we need to use the mind for decision-making and our day-to-day work. It helps us to:

- Solve problems
- Recall information
- Notice patterns
- Process emotions
- Make judgments, and more

This tool, which makes us feel inferior, is the same tool we need to survive in the physical world. We can't just leave the cup empty.

As I look around my kitchen, I notice that all the cups

either have a lid on them or they are turned upside down *when they are not being used.* Turning our cups upside down prevents others from pouring content into them as and when they like. Even if they do, however, no content will get into the cup when it is turned upside down. No one can turn it around except us. We control our own cup. Others can do so only if we allow it.

By keeping our cups empty, we can listen to what others are saying without reacting to their words. Also, being the master of our own cup means we have the choice to empty it, turn the mind on or off, whenever we like. Anytime we want to use our cup, we can turn it over and let it be filled up. After we use it, we pour away the content and turn it upside down again. A cup is just a tool, and we can put it aside whenever we choose.

Once we are awakened and realize who we really are, we cannot unrealize it. Even if our cup gets filled up unnoticed, we can empty it again when we regain consciousness. As long as we are aware that we are the masters — and we are using the mind and not the mind using us — then there are no issues. We don't have to resist the thoughts and emotions the mind produces; we can just let them be and observe them.

Observing Our Thoughts and Emotions

Thoughts and emotions produced by the mind are neither good nor bad. They are just mental habits, shortcuts created in the past. Even though they might not be true in the present, every time we resist them we are actually giving them more power and attention. We are showing the mind that it has control over us and can affect our happiness.

Our thoughts and emotions are powerless
until we give them power.

Real mastery isn't about forcing our cup to be empty or controlling the mind. Instead, it's just the opposite. It's about surrendering. Even though we have control over emptying our cup, we can't control the thoughts and emotions it produces. The subconscious mind produces thoughts automatically whenever it's triggered. Our body remembers the emotional pain we once felt no matter how hard we try to forget an event. But we can observe our thoughts and emotions, get the message they are trying to deliver, and let them go as they arise. As long as we don't cling to our thoughts and emotions, they cannot harm us.

Mastering the mind is about allowing it to do what it

is meant to do, while also allowing space between the mind and our conscious self. In other words, keeping the awareness that we are separate from the mind. Thoughts and emotions have no control over us when we are conscious of them.

I did an experiment to test out this theory. Being mindful of who I am, I asked my mind to attack me with the nastiest words it could find while I listened closely and wrote everything down. At first, my mind was really harsh. But after two minutes, or so, it ran out of ideas and got uncomfortable. It started squirming, as I waited to write down my next thoughts: *What else is there to criticize? Do I really need to continue? There is nothing else to say.*

Then, my mind began to repeat what it had said, and even contradicted itself. Finally, it gave up, saying: *I can't do this when you are staring at me.*

You can notice every thought and emotion, but you don't need to follow every single one of them.

Sometimes, our thoughts and emotions tell us something important. We can learn a great deal about how our past experiences shape our mental narrative. So observing this narrative and allowing it to surface is better than suppressing or resisting it, especially when it comes to emotions. After your observation, if you realize that they are irrelevant, you can always let them go later. Each moment is different. So at least listen to your thoughts and emotions without judgment first, and then decide what to do with them.

True masters don't argue with or blame their tools. They find ways to use their tools to the best of their capability. Mastering the mind is like teaching a child. When the child gets distracted and loses focus, *gently* pull them back to the main path instead of scolding them. The more you scold them, the more they will resist you. Likewise, the more we try to stop our thoughts, the more intrusive they become. When the mind starts to wander away, all we need to do is guide it home.

It's also pointless to blame ourselves for something we are not aware of. If we had known we were unconscious, we would have behaved differently. The thing is we didn't know.

Remaining Spiritually Awake

Awareness doesn't stay with us for very long. Unless we

can stay alert at all times, it's easy for us to be drawn into mental noise and let it take over. So how do we keep our alert awareness as long as possible?

Here are some suggestions that can help you remain spiritually awake:

1. Be one with nature more often.

Nature helps us to connect with our spiritual self. I couldn't help stopping to admire the beauty while I was climbing Mt. Batur in Bali, and when I walked along the path at Niagara Falls. But you don't need a holiday or expedition to enjoy nature. You can surround yourself with nature at home or at work.

One day, as I was working in my room, I turned my chair and noticed the view outside my window. The trees swaying from side to side in the wind without resistance mesmerized me. It was the first time I had felt so connected to nature since I had been awakened at the river. It reminded me of the calm and peaceful feelings I'd had during that experience. Since then, I have started paying more attention to nature; sometimes, I listen to the birds chirping in my neighborhood or watch the rain.

Plants and animals are good spiritual teachers; they

teach us a lot about stillness. You can have a pet or create a garden in your yard or indoors, but it's not necessary. Nature is all around us. It's not difficult to find, and it doesn't take too much time to connect with it. We just need to be aware of what's all around us.

2. Be mindful while doing simple activities like walking.

It's very easy to get lost in our thoughts while walking from one place to another, especially during the daily commute from home to work, and vice versa. The mind is already so familiar with the route that it tends to ignore the details of our surroundings.

There have been a few times, when I was about to reach home, and I had the realization that I didn't know what had happened from the moment I stepped out of the metro. Everything was so automatic. I had no awareness of my surroundings. If you were to ask me to describe the people who had walked past me, I wouldn't be able to tell you. I was so lost in my own thoughts. It's kind of scary to know we can be so unaware of what's right in front of us.

Do we really have so many things to think about? Do we really need to be thinking all day long? If we pay a little more attention to our feet touching the ground when we walk, we will feel more connected to the world. When we eat, we can choose to focus on the food and really savor the taste. Let walking be walking, and eating be eating. Don't let work, relationships, or anything else you are thinking about interfere with these simple, daily activities.

Perhaps breathing is the activity we most take for granted. It's so automatic that we hardly notice it at all. One of the best ways to stay awake and be aware is to focus on your breath and notice how your chest expands and contracts. You have access to your breath all the time, and it can remind you that you are alive.

3. Stop what you are doing every now and then.

To check in with the spiritual self, we can stop working every now and then, and take a mindfulness break. If at any given moment, we can't stop what we're doing, then it's a sign our minds have hooked us into our work and taken control of us. It means that completing the work (an event in the future) is more important than the present moment.

Being present is necessary for spiritual awareness. We lose our awareness when the mind takes us to somewhere in the future or the past. As an example, take the three *Survivor* castaways who suffered heatstroke. If they had stopped and become more aware of their situation, in the present moment, they would have noticed that their bodies couldn't cope with the heat and they needed to slow down. But because of their desire to win (a future event) coupled with their self-image of being strong (past conditioning), they failed to assess the situation properly.

Stopping what you're doing doesn't have to take too much time. It only takes a few seconds to reset your mind and be aware of yourself before taking further action.

Life is Full of Opportunities for Spiritual Practice

To be masters, we have to be learners, too. The best way to learn is from our mistakes. After recovering from depression, I became a tutor. Even though I was awakened, that didn't mean I was conscious all the time. There are still many events in my life that I can learn from and tutoring my students is one of them.

Here's an example. One evening, I was supposed to tutor a student. When I went to the student's house, she wasn't there. There was an event at her school and she couldn't make it back on time. This was the third time in two weeks a student had bailed on me. I knew it was unintentional; she had simply forgotten about her lesson. But as I was on the bus traveling back home, my chest began to tighten and then I felt anger that seemed to come out of nowhere. My mind began to play this story: *She made me wait. She could have told me earlier. I should demand that her mom pay me extra money for wasting my time traveling to her house.*

In the past, I would have either suppressed my anger or looped these angry thoughts in my head for quite a while. However, this time, I felt different. I was able to observe my thoughts from a third-party perspective. I was able to feel the impact of the anger on my body. I felt as though some of my cells came together and squeezed one another in a tight, little space. I was amazed by how detailed I felt the tension in my chest. But it didn't last very long. The anger dissolved immediately, once I noticed what was happening and let it go.

For the rest of my journey, I wondered: *Why did I feel angry? The parent was really sorry that her child didn't show up. The student didn't do it on purpose. Where did this anger come from?*

I already knew there was a subpersonality deep down inside my subconscious that always wanted me to stand up for myself and not get bullied. "He" didn't like it when others treated me like a pushover. "He" seemed to be on my side, and he acted like he wanted to protect me. However, he actually made me feel worse than a doormat. But up to that point in time, I didn't know where this subpersonality came from.

When I reached home and told my family about the incident, I finally realized my dad had conditioned me to feel this way! My dad reacted in exactly the same way as my subpersonality had reacted. He was angry and wanted me to ask for compensation. He expected me to be angry, too, for being taken advantage of. But when I wasn't, he perceived me as weak. It reminded me of all those times as a kid, when my dad wanted me to be angry and I refused. It was quite an epiphany.

In the end, everything went well, though. I didn't ask for compensation, and the student's parent paid me a little extra that month to make up for the transport fee.

We will still make mistakes, but after we are awakened it will be different.

Even though we have awakened, it doesn't mean we

are not vulnerable. We are not perfect, and we will make mistakes along the way, so we might as well turn them into spiritual practices. Every time you feel like you have made a mistake, use it as a reminder to reconnect with who you are and be aware of how your past experiences affect your thoughts, emotions, and body.

Any event in daily life can be turned into a spiritual practice. Some of mine include:

- When I'm waiting in line
- When my laptop restarts on its own
- When someone says something negative about me
- When I feel stuck in my work, and
- When I feel nervous talking to someone

Similar to a master in sports, who knows how to adjust himself to different competitors and circumstances, we need to learn how to connect with our spiritual selves regardless of where we are and what is happening around us.

Part of mastering the mind is to shorten the time it takes to become aware again. This requires continuous practice. The time between one moment of awareness and the next differs with individuals. Some of us might notice how we get carried away by the mind at least once every day. Some of us might be stuck with something we can't accept and go back to the previous stages. It might take us years until the next realization occurs.

Being mindful might be difficult, at first. But the more frequently we practice, the less time it will take to become aware again. The more we practice pouring away the content in our cup, the more we break our attachment to the cup and erode the old conditioning. So start small and expand your awareness slowly, until it pervades every second of your life.

Back to Empty

The cup's journey begins with emptiness, and it's only fitting to end with emptiness. No matter whether we are awakened or not, all cups face the same fate: they get emptied in the end when we die. No matter how beautiful our cup is, or how delicious the content, the cup is of no use when the master isn't there to use it.

When we were young, we didn't get to choose what we received in our empty cups, so we surrendered and let them get filled up. Society has its rules, and we learned those rules in order to survive in the physical world. No one is to be blamed. It's just a rite of passage that we must go through. However, when we are adults, we have a choice. We can either master our minds or let them run our lives.

Awakening is not only a gift, but also a choice.

It's up to us to decide if we want to continue with a cup-focused life, or empty our cups and begin again. Emptying the cup requires us to unlearn everything we have learned about ourselves previously and return the cup to its original state. Pouring away the content is to let go of the person we thought we were all these years. It's like being born for the second time. Just like when you were in your mother's womb, there is nothing much for you to do except trust the process and be aware of your aliveness.

This last stage is an invitation to be mindful of the spiritual self. It is not the end, but a new beginning, and all of us can renew ourselves when we decide to empty our individual cups.

Exercise: Test Your Mastery

Thoughts have no control over us when we are conscious of them. In this exercise, you are going to test how detached you are from the identity created by your mind.

Take out a pen and a piece of paper. Ask your mind to attack you with the nastiest words it can find. Don't filter or defend any of your thoughts. Simply observe them and write them down. Do you feel hurt by the criticism, or are you able to perceive these thoughts from a third-person perspective?

The thoughts in your mind that result in a reaction or feeling are beliefs you still hold about yourself. Be mindful of them and how they can affect your actions.

If you are not affected by the criticism, congratulations. You are starting to master your cup.

Conclusion

WHAT DOES IT MEAN TO LOVE YOURSELF?

If you are still looking for ways to love yourself or improve your self-esteem, you might have missed the point. You already are the love you are seeking. As a spiritual being, you and love are inseparable. Love cannot leave you. Love is ever-present. Love is you.

When we talk about loving ourselves, the "self" that most of us are referring to is the mind-made "self," also known as the "identity." This is different from loving your true self, the spiritual self.

The spiritual self doesn't need to be loved.

It is the source of love.

The only way you can learn to love your true self is to practice mindfulness. Recognize the space between your spiritual self and your mind. Empty everything you know about yourself and reconnect with your spiritual self.

You must also learn to love your mind, even though it is not your true self. The mind doesn't understand love. It only understands love as a mental concept. Love, to the mind, is based on beliefs, conditions, and expectations:

- *If I love myself, I shouldn't have any negative thoughts about myself.*
- *I can't love myself until I improve and fix myself.*
- *I'll love myself if other people love me.*
- *Loving myself is selfish.*
- *I'm not worthy of love. I don't deserve love.*

The mind can't grasp unconditional love. To the mind, we always need to do or achieve something before we can love or be loved. The mind is great for judging, analyzing, comparing ourselves with others, planning for the future, and remembering the past. But by doing so, we can also become trapped in endless loops and stories.

Whenever we feel the lack of self-love, instead of embracing this false belief, we can tap into the love that we already are and provide compassion to our minds. We can understand how our minds have been hurt in the past and uncover the mental patterns that are embedded deep within us. With awareness and compassion, we can help transcend the problems the mind has created for us. But we can only do this when we are detached from the mind and connected with our spiritual self.

The path to self-love isn't about developing a better identity or seeking love from others. This doesn't mean, however, that we can't improve ourselves, create a better self-image, or receive love from others. This is just not the basis for love anymore. We can still change our beliefs, think positively, and set goals for ourselves, but without mindfulness, it's easy to forget who we really are and get trapped in the pursuit.

There's this Buddhism quote, "No self, no problem." When there is no attachment to the mind-made identity, we will have no problem loving ourselves. Even though the mind does get in the way of our understanding our loving nature, we can learn to work with it.

When we understand from a deep knowingness that

we are pure love, our minds will naturally lose interest in judging others and us. It will interpret the action of others less, and we will feel more connected with them and ourselves, too.

Did You Like *Empty Your Cup*?

Thank you for purchasing my book and spending the time to read it.

Before you go, I'd like to ask you for a small favor. Could you please take a couple of minutes to leave a review for this book on Amazon?

Your feedback will not only help me grow as an author; it will also help those readers who need to hear the message in this book. So, thank you!

Please leave a review at www.nerdycreator.com/empty-your-cup.

Recommended Reading

To learn how to meditate, read these recommended books here: www.nerdycreator.com/bookclub/meditation/

Here are the other resources:
Change Your Thoughts - Change Your Life: Living the Wisdom of the Tao by Dr. Wayne Dyer; 2007; Hay House, Carlsbad, California.

Morty Lefkoe's Natural Confidence online course

Self-Compassion: The Proven Power of Being Kind to Yourself by Kristen Neff; 2015; William Morrow/Harper Collins, New York, New York.

The Power of Now: A Guide to Spiritual Enlightenment by Eckhart Tolle; 2004; Namaste Publishing, Vancouver, BC, Canada.

The Shift: Taking Your Life from Ambition to Meaning by Dr. Wayne Dyer; 2010; Hay House, Carlsbad, California.

A New Earth: Awakening to Your Life's Purpose by Eckhart Tolle; 2005; Penguin Books, New York, New York.

Peace Is Every Breath: A Practice for Our Busy Lives by Thich Nhat Hanh; 2011; HarperCollins Publishers, New York, New York.

Here are more books by Yong Kang:
The Emotional Gift: Memoir of a Highly Sensitive Person Who Overcame Depression

Fearless Passion: Find the Courage to Do What You Love

To see the latest books by the author, please go to www.nerdycreator.com/books.

About the Author

Yong Kang Chan, best known as Nerdy Creator, is a blogger, online teacher, and private tutor. Having low self-esteem growing up, he has read a lot of books on personal growth, psychology, and spirituality.

Based in Singapore, Yong Kang teaches mathematics and accounting to his students. On his website, he writes blog posts on self-compassion and mindfulness to help introverts and people with low self-esteem.

Please visit his website at www.nerdycreator.com.

Made in the USA
San Bernardino, CA
26 January 2020